T0365862

TURN OF THE
TWENTIETH

**Early 1900s Northern New England Through
The Lens Of Photographer Glenduen Ladd**

SUSAN ZIZZA

DEDICATION

*To Beverly Uran, whose devotion to preserving artist
Glenduen Ladd's work made this book possible.*

REFERENCES

Advent Christian Church Official Website, www.adventchristian.org.
Emigrant's Directory and Guide, Francis Evans, 1832.
Encyclopaedia Britannica, www.britannica.com.
Historical New Hampshire, Volume 50, Richard Hamilton, New Hampshire Historical Society,1995.
History of Compton County, L.L. Channell, 1886.
King Phillip's Territory, Everett Wiswell, 1976.
This Fabulous Century, Sixty Years of American Life, Volume I, TIME-LIFE BOOKS, 1969.
The Grand Resort Hotels of the White Mountains, A Vanishing Architectural Legacy,
Bryant F. Tolles, Jr., David R. Godine, Publisher, 1998.
Tales Told in the Shadow of the White Mountains, Charles J. Jordan, University Press of New England, 2003.
The Boys of '76; A History of the Battles of the Revolution, Charles Carleton Coffin, Harper & Brothers, 1876.
The Colebrook Cookbook, Revised Bicentennial Edition, 1980.
Townships Heritage WebMagazine, Townshippers Association, www.townshipsheritage.com.

Layout Designer: Jerome Cuyos

To order additional copies of this book, contact:
Xlibris
844-714-8691
www.Xlibris.com
Orders@Xlibris.com

ISBN: Softcover   978-1-4257-7567-4
           Hardcover   978-1-4363-0997-4
           EBook   978-1-4771-7204-9

Library of Congress Control Number: 2007909849

Print information available on the last page

Rev. date: 06/15/2024

TABLE OF CONTENTS

In this 1910 photo, Glenduen is probably holding a No. 3A Folding Pocket Kodak Model B-2 camera that sold for about $20. According to vintage camera expert Rob Niederman, "it was produced from June 1904, to November 1906, and made 3 ¼ x 5 ½ inch 'postcard' images on 122-roll film. The No. 3A FPK series was introduced in May 1903, and discontinued in 1915. It was extraordinarily popular and over 360,000 were sold."

ACKNOWLEDGMENTS

This book could not have been written without North Country native Beverly (Hunt) Uran's dedication in preserving the art, photography and memorabilia of her aunt, 19th century-born artist Glenduen Ladd. Beverly, along with her daughter Judy (Hunt) Cardinal, was invaluable as a resource regarding Glenduen's life and work and generous in sharing her recollections, as well as her archives.

Old Hall Stream Cemetery Trustee Cheryl Clogston proved to be a great aid, providing documentation regarding the restoration of Old Hall Stream Cemetery and her own memories of Glenduen.

I spent a wonderful afternoon with the late Neil Tillotson, former Tillotson Corporation industrialist and owner of the Balsams Grand Resort, who dropped his busy schedule (at 102, his day was still filled with business appointments) and took me on a tour of his birthplace of Hereford and the cemetery he helped Glenduen restore.

Thanks must go to Patty (Ladd) McAllister for allowing me to delve into her grandmother, Grace Ladd's trunk and loaning me the fragile letters and scrapbooks that had been tucked away for nearly six decades.

I am grateful to antique dealers Kellyann and Mark Yelle of Potato Barn Antiques in Northumberland, New Hampshire, for assistance in providing details of turn-of-the-twentieth-century life portrayed by the vintage photographs.

Much credit is due the dedicated library staff at town, state and university levels, on both sides of the border, in helping with the documentation for this book. I owe much, also, to the meticulous proofreading skills of Barbara Larssen, Ellie Gooch and Joan Chase.

Words cannot express my appreciation to Morgan Rockhill, of Morgan Rockhill PhotoDigital, for his generosity in allowing me use of his state-of-the art camera and computerized equipment to reproduce the photographs. His patience and willingness to share his knowledge of digital design was invaluable in my learning how to digitally repair photographs without compromising the images' artistic integrity.

Thanks also go to Charlie and Donna Jordan, publishers of the **Colebrook Chronicle** and **Lancaster Herald,** for helping this book along in its infancy by printing several chapters as a serial in their publication, **Northern New Hampshire Magazine.** The cover design was inspired by a suggestion Charlie made for the series' artwork.

This project has been made easier by the support of my friends and family, especially that of my husband, Mark. He kept me on balance with his sense of humor and practical good sense. His patience as a sounding board never faltered.

"I thought you'd be interested in taking a look at these," said my visitor, gently easing her armful of vintage photo albums onto my kitchen table.

As a writer and photographer for newspapers and magazines in northern New England for over 20 years, I had become known for my interest in local history, particularly that involving the Victorian era and the early years of the 20th century. As a result, I had often been approached by people with tales to tell or old photos to show, such as the ones brought to me by North Country native Beverly Uran that fine spring day. Those photos had been taken by her aunt, Glenduen Wells Ladd, a regionally well-known artist born at the turn of the century.

After Beverly had left, I brought the books up to my office for a closer look. Seated cross-legged on the carpet, I pulled an album from the pile of half a dozen stacked around me. Penned across the cover were the words, "To 1919," containing photos dating from 1907 to 1919. Slowly turning pages fragile with age, I gazed at the images taken nearly a century past. I was struck by the subjects of the photos, quite different from the usual images of hardy loggers in spiked boots, rugged farmers behind plows, and roughly clad children in front of one-room schoolhouses; images so cleverly lighted and composed that they appeared vibrantly alive, as if the shutter had been clicked minutes instead of a century ago.

I stopped, my hand arrested over one photo of a girl on a grassy bank with roofs and chimneys looming in the distance at the horizon's edge. With its odd angle and slightly dark aura, the image tugged at my mind's edge. What did it remind me of? Then, I remembered. Andrew Wyeth and that famous painting he had done of his neighbor. What was it called? Yes, that was it, "Christina's World." I turned the photo over and read the date written across the back—1917. It was the year that Wyeth (whose art reflected so well the rock-ribbed spirit of northern New England) was born.

As daylight faded into night, I remained absorbed as one image after another drew me in to a world far removed from the one pressing in on me from my office window. Reaching the bottom of the pile, I slid out a worn, leather-bound ledger. Opening it, I saw tiny hard-to-decipher script marching across page after page. It was a daily journal, spanning 17 years, penned by the photographer's grandmother—detailing life at the turn of the 20th century on a homestead carved out of the deep forest surrounding the town of Pittsburg, New Hampshire.

That day in May 2000, created in me a strong desire to preserve and share this artist's unique perspective of her world at the turn of the 20th century. To reproduce and restore the photographs, as well as research the stories behind them, was a task entailing several years labor. It was my aim to preserve the integrity of the photos—limiting retouching to such minor changes as the removal of age spots or repairing cracks. They have been reproduced as originally composed, without cropping. I have also included examples of Glenduen's artwork, especially scenes evocative of rural northern New England.

Besides the photos and paintings, I was assisted in my research by the contents of a trunk from the attic of a farmhouse in Stewartstown. It had lain virtually untouched since the death of Glenduen's mother-in-law, Grace, in 1945, and contained letters, news and obituary clippings dating from the 1880s. I spent one entire winter on this literary treasure hunt, poring over the faded documents and peeling back the years to reveal what had once been life in the North Country.

The treasure hunt is over, my journey is done. Yours can now begin. So sit back while I tell you the tale of a northern New England woman's "Turn of the Twentieth" world. I hope you enjoy the trip as much as I did.

—Susan Zizza

Glenduen, with an eye for the unusual, chose this whimsical 1922 pose of her uncle, George Keysar, in suit and straw boater, nonchalantly perched atop a pulp pile stretching to the horizon. Glenduen Ladd collection.

The perspective and slightly dark aura of this 1917 shot is reminiscent of realist painter Andrew Wyeth's famous work, "Christina's World." Wyeth, born in the same year as this photo was taken, had a summer home in Maine. He was as adept at capturing the essence of rock-ribbed northern New England with his brush, as was Glenduen with her camera. Glenduen Ladd photo.

Artist and photographer Glenduen Ladd, serene and self-possessed at 19 years of age (1910). Glenduen Ladd collection.

"Painting is silent poetry," observed the Greek philosopher Plutarch. The young artist serenely gazing out from a fragile, nearly century-old photograph, has the eyes of a poet. Though her image is fading with the passage of time, Glenduen Ladd's eyes are as mesmerizing as Mona Lisa's smile. So are the images contained within the pages of **Turn of the Twentieth.**

Most of the photographs and all of the paintings are from the collection of Glenduen Ladd, born in northern New Hampshire on December 19, 1891, nearly a decade before the dawn of a new century. She died on May 1, 1983 at the age of 91. Although Glenduen, a professional artist, was largely known for her paintings of North Country scenes, she was also an amateur photographer, whose compelling images chronicle early 20th century life in northern New England, preserving for posterity the passing of an era. She had an eye for the unusual and her photographs provide intriguing footnotes to North Country history—the rescue of a Revolutionary soldier's grave and those of other early settlers in a Canadian border hamlet; the Adventist movement that spread north after the "Great Disappointment;" and the colorful frontiersmen of the northern forest.

Included in the albums are photos of a youthful Glenduen, who often composed the photograph, before stepping in front of the camera. She can be seen—dressed in the best fashions of the day—peeking behind a tree or wrapped in fur as she and her beau prepare for a winter's sleigh ride and kneeling in her flower garden. The compositions from Glenduen's collection exude charm, grace and a great sense of fun.

Glenduen's oil paintings have a similar impact. Her landscapes project a softness that is reminiscent of the scenes in M-G-M's 1954 musical, "Brigadoon." This film told the tale of an enchanted town which remained unchanging and invisible to the outside world except for one day every hundred years. There, where time had stopped, a mist settled over hill and dale, muting the greens and blues of grass and sky. With the stroke of her brush, Glenduen achieved the same glow. Her oil paintings still retain the magical power of holding the viewer within the grasp of a bygone day—water rushing over the wheel of a mill or a church spire silhouetted against the softened mauve and gold of a wintry sunset.

Glenduen revealed her own nostalgia for the era into which she was born through her art, photographs and scrapbooks. She was a great fan of cartoonist Erwin L. Hess and saved many clippings from his series, "The Good Old Days." One cartoon has the caption, "Moments we'd like to live over again." Over these words, Hess drew a winter scene of horses pulling a sleighful of children along a moonlit road. "Another New Year's here!" exclaims the father to his wife. "1900! How time flies!"

Time must have truly flown for Glenduen. The word, "busy," doesn't seem an adequate enough adjective to describe this artist who produced a prodigious amount of work in her lifetime. Her artistic nature also revealed itself in her beautifully decorated homes and extensive flower gardens. She was proficient as a seamstress, repaired antique chinaware, decorated elaborate cakes for weddings and played the piano, accordion and mandolin. These achievements were accomplished by a person who never went further than the eighth grade.

Glenduen's driving need to create surfaced at an early age. In an interview she gave in 1975, at the age of 84, she told Manchester

Sunday News feature writer Earl Burton that she could recall drawing pictures from a farm journal while sitting in a high chair. One of her early artistic efforts was a pencil cartoon drawn in 1906 on a penny postcard bearing President McKinley's stamped likeness. She was 15 years old when she began using oils, but her compulsion to create led her to experiment with mediums of all types, including pencil, watercolors, and charcoal. Just about anything at hand served as a canvas for her landscapes, floral stills and animal life—the cupboards in her kitchen, china ware, farm implements and pieces of forest fungus. Even in her final years at the Coös County Nursing Hospital in West Stewartstown, she continued to bring to life the images which flowed from her still-imaginative mind.

At the end of her life, as she sat in her chair or lay in her bed at the county hospital, she would draw impish pixies on egg cartons and give them to visitors. Nurses and doctors who attended her would often find their medicine cups handed back to them, covered with delightful scenes which flew from her clever fingers.

Those who own pieces of Beecher Falls factory furniture dating from the first half of the 20th century may well find that they also own a piece of Ladd art. For 30 years, 15 of them as head decorator, she worked painting designs on bedroom and dining room sets at what is now known as the Beecher Falls, Vermont Division of Ethan Allen.

In her later years, she particularly enjoyed painting New England scenes. Her landscape of Percy Peaks in Stratford was on exhibit for many years in the Public Service of New Hampshire office in Colebrook. In the 1970s, she donated a painting of Percy Peaks to the Upper Connecticut Valley Hospital in Colebrook, where it remains to this day. The hospital was a cherished charity of the artist, who donated funds generated by her paintings to the Ladies' Auxiliary. She told the **Sunday News** reporter, "When you give to a church, you help only one denomination. When you give to a hospital, you help people of all denominations."

Covered bridges were a favorite subject, including the bridge over the Saco River in Conway, New Hampshire, and a bridge in Lyndon, Vermont. A New York tourist commissioned her to paint Beaver Brook Falls in Colebrook, one of the most beautiful attractions in the area.

Although Glenduen has been gone for over two decades, she remains a local luminary, largely due to the paintings which can still be found in North Country homes. Mention her name, particularly to those of the older generation, and their faces light up. They'll proudly show off the pieces they own or if they don't own any, tell enviously of others who do. Her work is so valued that it is nearly impossible to convince those fortunate enough to own an example of her handiwork to part with it. However, as is the case with much of northern New Hampshire's heritage, little by little her work is leaving the area through estate sales and auctions.

Glenduen tinted photographs for photographer Edward Paquette of Beecher Falls, Vermont, but she never became a professional photographer. Still, if painting was a passion, it could be said that photography was her obsession. Glenduen always had her camera ready and compelled family and friends to serve as models in the living portraits she created. Her photography, for the most part, was carefully choreographed, with great attention given to scenery, costumes, and props. Years later, her nearly fanatical devotion to detail remained intact. After she had painted an autumn river scene from a post card, one person actually visited the spot and counted the rocks to see if Glenduen's painting was authentic. Beverly Uran relates, "She had painted every one."

A pixie-like sense of humor pervades many of her photographs, such as the shot of beau Harry Ladd and friend in drag. While the older members of her family seemed to get into the spirit of things, her younger models, which she chose from among an abundant supply of nieces and nephews, were not always enthusiastic about dressing up and being ordered about by their autocratic aunt. "I got so I used to hate to see her coming, with her great, big flash bulbs," wryly recalls her niece, Beverly. How were they to know that their aunt was capturing on film a cherished way of life that would be all but gone by the end of the 20th century?

Despite her amateur status, Glenduen achieved the same results with her camera as she had with her brush. Her images are powerful, a step back in time to an enchanted land—the "good old days" of the North Country.

The year 1909, in Belmont. Her sister Hazel in the forefront, a mischievous eighteen-year-old Glenduen peeks behind a tree. Glenduen Ladd collection.

Snug and warm under a bearskin rug, Glenduen, with her dapper beau and future husband, Harry Ladd, prepares for a sleigh ride along the snowy streets of Colebrook on March 17, 1911. Glenduen Ladd collection.

Glenduen kneels in a gown of lawn (a light linen or cotton material) tending her flower garden in the summer of 1913. Glenduen Ladd collection.

Glenduen (right, with her sister Hazel) was already showing artistic promise by the time she reached four years old. Glenduen Ladd collection.

Glenduen's niece, Judy Cardinal, still has this foot-high mushroom with drawings evoking life in the great northern forest. Susan Zizza photo.

Glenduen (center) with her crew at the Beecher Falls Factory in 1924. She served as head decorator for 15 years. On the back of this photo were inscribed just the first names of those in the photo: Harold A., Henry, Palmyra, Antoinette, Yvonne, Elizabeth, Mae, Mary, Peg, Eva, Iola and Louise. Glenduen Ladd collection.

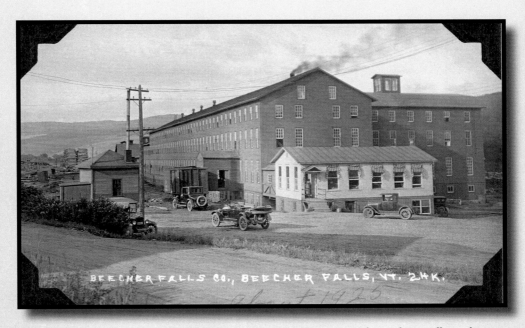

Postcard of the Beecher Falls Factory (circa 1925), now the Ethan Allen plant in Beecher Falls, Vermont. Glenduen Ladd collection.

These ladies, appearing particularly North Country strong and stern, are actually Harry Ladd and friend in drag. Elegantly hatted and muffed, these two look ready to pummel with purses any fashion critics at hand (1915). Glenduen Ladd photo.

Chapter I

CHILDREN OF A NEW CENTURY
Striking a Pose

Grace Arlene, the daughter of woodsman and lawman Harold Carbee, was a frequent subject of Glenduen's photography sessions, perhaps because of her natural demeanor in front of a camera, even at a young age. As these photos show, some of Glenduen's other models weren't as enthusiastic about posing on a hot summer day in their Sunday best.

The children of Harry Ladd's sister, Della Carbee: Grace, with brothers Ladd and Sherwood, whose faces say it all. Grace appears cool and unperturbed in a white cotton dress with eyelet trim; the boys, less contentedly, in belted tunics and knickers. Sherwood is also holding a water witching stick probably taken from an apple tree. Apple and cherry trees were considered among the best material for dowsing sticks. Glenduen Ladd photo.

On July 18, 1913, toddler Grace Carbee has an affectionate hug for a compliant kitty at her grandmother, Grace Ladd's farm in Stewartstown. Glenduen Ladd photo.

Grace Carbee, in a bloomer dress with dropped waist, gazes into the camera against the backdrop of a rope portiere in this 1915 photo. Glenduen Ladd photo.

A young gardener, knee-deep in her flower garden, gives a copious bath to a thirsty plant with her miniature watering can. By the time this photo was taken in 1937, little girls' dresses had shortened considerably. Glenduen Ladd photo.

Kathryn Hall in a homemade bathing suit made from stockings, combines pleasure and practicality with a dab of fishing in the midst of her August swim at Averill Lake in Vermont. Glenduen Ladd photo.

Chapter II

GIBSON GIRL GOES NORTH
Fashions, Frills and Furbelows

Far from the urban centers of fashion, with only the Sears Roebuck catalogue and Buttrick patterns to rely on, the young women of the far north managed to stay abreast of the latest in ladies' wear. Although some of their clothing was "off the peg," that is, ready-made, many of the young ladies made their own clothes or hired the services of a local seamstress. Glenduen herself was an accomplished needlewoman. With her talents and innate sense of style, she was much in demand and would stay several weeks at a time at homes of friends and neighbors sewing an entire trousseau for the coming season or for the wardrobe of a college-bound student.

The Gibson girl, created by magazine illustrator Charles Dana Gibson, was the ideal that women strove to emulate from the 1890s to the First World War. "The Gibson Girl was the image of the professional woman during the 'teens," explains fashion historian Kellyann Yelle of Northumberland's Potato Barn Antiques. She added that their intricate hairdos were created with the aid of a "rat." A rat was made with hair pulled from a woman's brush that was stored in a hair receiver as part of her dresser set. It would then be rolled in nets of various shapes and the woman would loop her hair over the "rat" to give her hair a thicker appearance.

According to the book, **This Fabulous Century Volume I**, the public's imagination was caught by Gibson's pen and ink drawings of a haughty, very lovely and beautifully dressed young woman who graced the pages of serials that ran in the old humor magazine, **Life**, from October 1900 to July 1901. It wasn't the intention of the artist, who considered himself a satirical cartoonist, to make a fashion statement. Nevertheless, the lovely lady coming to life under Gibson's pen became the model for women to follow in dress, hairstyle and even in manner. The Gibson influence spread even into the northern reaches of New England, as the accompanying photographs show.

Millinery shops did a booming business with the demand for excessively decorative hats. Feathers, ribbons and even fruit, made from such fine material as brocade, chiffon, velvet, lace, silk and satin, could be seen atop the heads of well-dressed young ladies (1911). Glenduen Ladd collection.

Alma Owen (surname later Drew, then Colby), in a crisp white cotton and beribboned sailor dress, feeds a fawn in this peaceful 1911 pastoral scene. Glenduen Ladd photo.

"Ready For Church" is written on this 1910 photo of Glenduen and her friend, schoolteacher Bernice Moore, taken in Belmont. Glenduen accented her hat with a peacock feather and displays a daring new skirt length. Skirts still covered a lady's ankles and Glenduen's exposure of several inches of ankle was noted in the writer's added comment, "You see g. wears her skirts pretty short!" Glenduen Ladd collection.

Garbed in a velvet-trimmed gown, Lettie McClellan (surname later Hall, then Davis), gazes out over the Connecticut River into New Hampshire from her high perch on Canaan Hill in Vermont (1915). Glenduen Ladd photo.

1911. A pensive Lettie McClellan in striped cotton gown and framed by ivy. Glenduen Ladd photo.

Friend Lettie, clothed in a silk waistcoat and stiff-standing lace collar, absorbed in her book. The table is covered with a beautiful Battenburg-looking lace tablecloth (1918). Glenduen Ladd photo.

Chapter III

MOVE OVER FOR THE MOTOR CAR

Buggies Bumped
By the Auto

By the early 1900s, American's love affair with the automobile was in full swing. As the book **This Fabulous Century Volume I** reveals, America had only 8,000 cars in 1900. But, by 1912, New Hampshire alone boasted at least 4,013 registered vehicles, as seen by the license plate on one of this chapter's photos. The arrival of this new and more aggressive means of transport required an entirely new line of clothing—long dusters to protect elegant suits and dresses; a variety of headgear for men; and netting for the women to protect their bedecked bonnets and carefully crafted hairdos. In good weather, families fortunate enough (or reckless enough, from some of their neighbors' viewpoint) to own one of these contrivances piled into touring cars to travel the countryside and visit family and friends. Still, in the dawning decades of the new century, horse-drawn conveyances were still a popular and practical means of getting around the North Country.

Smartly attired in a warm suit with wide, checkered lapels, Glenduen prepares for a buggy ride with Patch, Harry Ladd's prize horse. Glenduen Ladd collection.

George Hancock leans lazily against his team of oxen, in this 1910 shot. Precursors to the tractor-trailers, oxen were used to transport goods to far-flung corners of the northern forests. A regular run was the Colebrook to Portland, Maine, route. Glenduen Ladd photo.

The gentle face of ox team driver George Hancock, who makes a fashion statement of his own in striped cotton shirt and denim overalls. Glenduen Ladd photo.

In 1915, a six-horse team pulls a snow-roller over country roads with their drivers, Norman Hall and Harry Ladd, almost indistinguishable under heavy wraps. Glenduen Ladd photo.

Young Marjorie Perkins (who did not survive childhood) and Glenduen in front of that new-fangled invention, the automobile. Only 8,000 autos were registered in the United States by 1900. When Henry Ford began producing an affordable vehicle, the first Model T coming off the line at the Piquette plant in Detroit in 1908, ownership swiftly increased. By the time of this photo, 1912, New Hampshire alone had at least 4,013, as evidenced by the license number. Glenduen Ladd collection.

A family ready to set out and show off their Model T touring car. The four-door, five passenger model was very popular and often came with a convertible top that folded down behind the back seat. Glenduen Ladd photo.

Glenduen and Harry, out for a ride, show off their motoring clothes. The well-turned out motorist never left for a trip without a long coat known as a duster to protect the elegant fashions underneath. Headgear included netting for the ladies to protect their elaborate hairdos and hats. Men topped their outfits with bowlers or caps. Glenduen Ladd collection.

Chapter IV

SOUVENIERS OF SUMMERING IN STYLE

Playing Cards Recall Glory of Grand Hotels

A century-old deck of cards that once sold as a souvenir now helps tell the story of the golden age of the grand hotels of the White Mountains. Many of the hotels gracing the face of these cards have passed into history.

Historians consider the era of the White Mountain grand hotels to be a brief one, less than half a century in length—from about 1875 to just before World War I. Although the glory days of the grand old ladies of the North Country are gone, the souvenir industry this era generated helped secure its place in history.

The New Hampshire Historical Society sponsored an exhibit in 1998 (at its Museum of New Hampshire in Concord) of the grand hotel era. Titled "Popular Resorts: Grand Hotels of the White Mountains," it included a unique sample of the hotel souvenir industry in its traveling version of the exhibit—a deck of cards published by Chisholm Brothers in Portland, Maine. At the same time, the Society deemed it appropriate to make a reproduction of the cards

to raise funds for its continued effort to preserve and promote the history of the Granite State.

Originally, the cards' faces had four colors—peach, blue, green and tan. Former curator Hilary Anderson and former museum store manager Rebecca Courser, who oversaw the re-creation of the cards, decided to go with one color, tan, to avoid anyone confusing the reproduction with the real thing. The reproduction also only contains 52 views. The original added a picture to the face of the Joker in the deck, the Tip-Top House on Mount Washington.

Beverly Uran has a set of the century-old cards which once belonged to her aunt, Glenduen Ladd. "Among The White Mountains Souvenir Cards—53 Principal Views of the White Mountains of New Hampshire," proclaims the embossed gold letters on the back of the royal blue colored card holder.

On the face of each card is a different picture of well-known White Mountain attractions taken from photographs which were reduced to fit the space. Displayed on the back of the cards is an artist's rendering of what, perhaps, was once the most famous New Hampshire attraction of all—the Profile of Franconia Notch. The Old Man is surrounded by a flower border of delicate Alpine Sandwort, which, declares the publishers, "only grows above the timber line, in the region of perpetual snows." In each of the cards' four corners is a reproduction of the New Hampshire State Seal.

A goodly portion of the cards depict resorts, many of them now only a memory: Grays Inn in Jackson, Fabyan House, the Sinclair in Bethlehem, Intervale House, the Waumbek Hotel in Jefferson, Deer Park Hotel in North Woodstock, the Kearsage in North Conway, Crawford House, Mt. Pleasant House and Franconia's Profile House.

Several railroad scenes are shown—the Crawford House Railroad Station, Frankenstein's Trestle and the Great Cut in Crawford Notch and Jacob's Ladder on Mt. Washington. The cards were sold on trains as well as at hotels and helped to ease the boredom of what was about a five-hour train ride to the White Mountains from the cities of New York, Boston and Portland.

The marketing of hotels by means of souvenirs was mostly done by railroad companies and energetic independent entrepreneurs. According to a 1995 article in the New Hampshire Historical Society's periodical, **Historical New Hampshire,** by Richard Hamilton, marketing was not something that hotel companies did well themselves. The book notes that a search of the **New York Times** between 1875 and 1895 found only the Glen House, Waumbek Hotel, Profile House and Barron family resorts at Bretton Woods doing any advertising.

Companies such as Charles Pollach & Sons of Boston produced a plethora of small, easily portable woodenware objects for tourists to bring home, including boxes, pin cushions, letter openers, cooking timers, needle holders,

booklet covers, pens, bookmarks, snuff boxes and napkin rings.

The Chisholm Brothers, who were billed on the card holder as "publishers and R.R. news contractors," also produced guidebooks and special booklets containing dried, mounted Alpine flowers. The Summit House ordered 326 12-page booklets in July 1888, at the cost of 25 cents each. One edition was for the White Mountain district and one centered on flowers growing on Mount Washington. As author Richard Hamilton wryly observes, "Apparently there were no environmental concerns in those days."

To attract passengers, railroad companies published guidebooks to the resorts served by their trains and the White Mountains were high on the list of tourist destinations. The Chisholm Brothers were one of the companies contracted to produce many of those guidebooks and these guidebooks became souvenirs themselves. One invoice from Chisholm, states Hamilton, shows that the cost of a guidebook was minimal—only 15 cents apiece in 1888. Not a bad price for tourists, he points out, who were paying from $8 to $15 a day on the American plan at places like the Maplewood Hotel or the Sinclair House.

The fortunes of the grand hotels rose and fell with the railroads. When America transferred its affections to the automobile, rail travel for leisure began a long decline. Americans were on the move, free to travel as they wished and not as apt to spend an entire summer at resorts in the far northern reaches of New Hampshire.

As they aged and fell into disuse, some of the grand hotels succumbed to fire, like the Crawford House, the Kearsage, the Waumbek, Maplewood and the Profile House. Others were razed, like the Mt. Pleasant House and still more were converted to other uses. After being rebuilt three times following fires, Gray's Inn struggled on as a youth camp, but a fire in 1983 dealt the fourth structure a final blow. The site of the Profile House is now a state park; the nine-hole course at the Kearsage became the heart of the North Conway Country Club.

Sadly, even the Old Man in Franconia Notch no longer exists. During the early hours of May 3, 2003, its granite profile slid off Cannon Mountain, blending anonymously into the rubble of the mountain's hillside.

However, two of the hotels featured on the cards are flourishing into the 21st century—the Mount Washington Hotel in Bretton Woods and the Balsams Resort in Dixville. Surviving the Depression and bankruptcy, the Balsams Grand Resort defied the odds and is a thriving tourist destination today. The Mount Washington Hotel celebrated its 100th birthday in 2002, with probably the biggest bash the old dame had ever seen. And the Sleeping Beauty of the North Country, the Mountain View Grand in Whitefield, came to life in May of 2002, with a dedication ceremony that drew media and luminaries from far and wide.

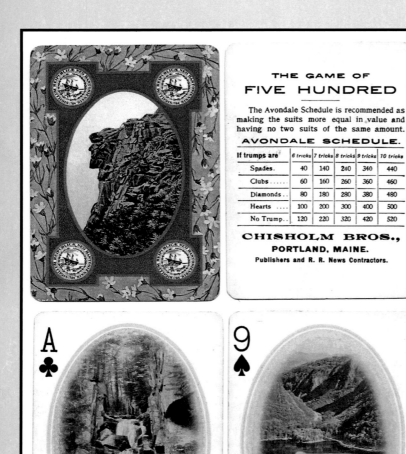

THE GAME OF
FIVE HUNDRED

The Avondale Schedule is recommended as making the suits more equal in value and having no two suits of the same amount.

AVONDALE SCHEDULE.

If trumps are	6 tricks	7 tricks	8 tricks	9 tricks	10 tricks
Spades.	40	140	240	340	440
Clubs	60	160	260	360	460
Diamonds ..	80	180	280	380	480
Hearts	100	200	300	400	500
No Trump..	120	220	320	420	520

CHISHOLM BROS.,
PORTLAND, MAINE.
Publishers and R. R. News Contractors.

THE FLUME, DIXVILLE NOTCH, N.H.

LAKE GLORIETTE AND THE BALSAMS, DIXVILLE NOTCH, N.H.

Clockwise, from top left—the Old Man of Franconia Notch backs every card; rules to Five Hundred, America's most popular card game in the early 20th century, introduced in 1904, by the United States Playing Card Company, according to the company's website (it is a combination of Euchre and Bridge); the Flume in Dixville Notch (a miniature of the one in Franconia); and The Balsams Grand Hotel overlooking Lake Gloriette in Dixville. Glenduen Ladd collection.

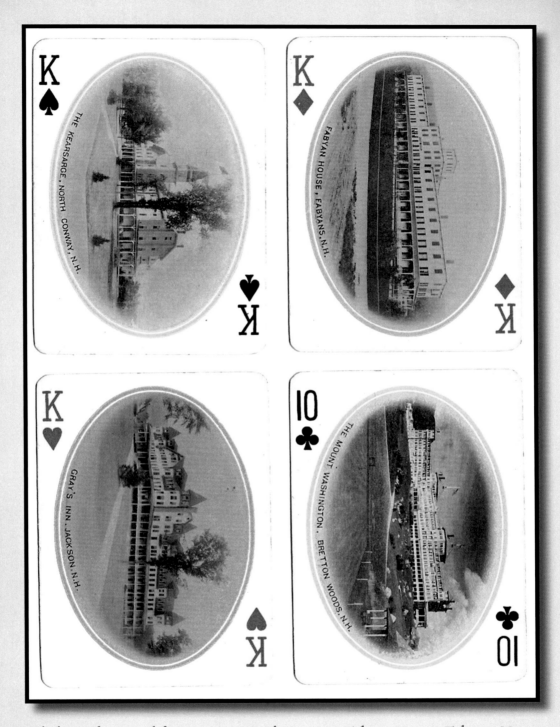

Clockwise from top left, Kearsage, North Conway; Fabyan House, Fabyan; Mount Washington Hotel, Bretton Woods; Gray's Inn, Jackson. These are just a few of the grand hotels featured on souvenir playing cards published by Chisholm Bros., Portland, Maine.

On The Canvas

Paintings By Glenduen Ladd

Glenduen's soft brush strokes preserved for posterity the pastoral scenes of her youth. Her work, of prolific proportions, include the art displayed on the following pages: a winter scene; a country road, with Mt. Chocorua in the southern White Mountains as a backdrop; a covered bridge in Lyndon, Vermont; Dixie Dam on the Swift Diamond River in Dixville; and a still life that earned Glenduen sixth place in a national competition.

The melancholy of this 1973 painting (seen below), of an abandoned barn atop Meriden Hill in Columbia, seems to reflect the artist's feelings on the inexorable decline of farming in New England.

Chapter V

FARMING ON THE 45TH PARALLEL

Ledger of A Life—Diary
From 1890-1907

In the remote northern town of Clarksville, New Hampshire, a ribbon of a road cuts sharply away from Route 3 and rises steadily from the upper Connecticut River valley floor. At the height of the rise, just a few hundred feet away from the sign which proclaims that the traveler has arrived at the 45th parallel, is a small clearing. That clearing, where now rests a modern ranch-style house, is the site of Glenduen (Wells) Ladd's childhood home. It was here, on December 19, 1891, halfway between the North Pole and the equator, that she was born.

The birth of Horace and Jennie (Keysar) Wells' second child received one line in Marinda (Hart) Keysar's journal. Glenduen's grandmother was a woman of few words, at least on paper. "Jennie's baby was born, I stayed with her a week," wrote Marinda, who lived with her husband, Dudley, on a farm in Pittsburg. Although there was plenty of space in the large ledger where she made her entries, Marinda rarely used more than one or two lines. The happy occasion of her daughter Kate's wedding a few weeks before

Glenduen's birth had prompted an extravagant outburst of four lines in celebration. More often, Marinda's carefully cramped style of writing reflected a lifetime of having to economize both time and resources.

Marinda began her journal on January 1, 1890, and continued it for the first 15 years of her granddaughter's life. From the now yellowed pages of this 100-year-old ledger, a vivid picture emerges of rural life in northern New England at the cusp of a new century. The passing of the seasons provided a steady rhythm to Marinda's life and that of her husband, Dudley, five daughters, Isabelle, Kate, Jennie, Etta, Mary and son George.

The dates covering the house-bound months of winter are filled with comments about the weather, sewing circles, prayer meetings, sleigh rides to visit neighbors, holiday gatherings and nights of sitting with sick family and friends. Marinda also used this time for projects such as papering the parlor.

The weather seems to have been as capricious as it is today. On New Year's Eve in 1897, it snows a foot. "No roads anywhere," writes Marinda. Another blizzard follows on January 3, with temperatures dipping to 20 below on January 4. A week later, it's pouring.

A true January thaw causes havoc in 1906. On January 24 of that year, Marinda writes, "Snow gone and wagons running. (Son-in-law) Jerre came near to getting drowned in the road on the way to the Falls." A blizzard in 1906 was worthy of special mention. "Snowed two feet in three hours," she notes on February 8.

In the spring came the "freshet," the rush of water coming off mountain streams and filling rivers to overflowing. "A terrible freshet," she writes in 1892. "The dams and everything are broke loose." The following spring she makes this entry, "The river men are plenty around. The water is so high they can't work."

Spring also meant sugaring time to tap the farm's stand of maple trees. "(Son) George broke into the sugar place today," Marinda writes on April 1, 1898. "The snow was five feet deep." In 1890, it was her husband, referred to in her journal as simply D., who shoveled off the roof one early April day and "hooped" the buckets.

On April 3, after feeding the work hands dinner and "washing down the schoolhouse," Marinda herself "went down on a load of logs" to tap the sugar. "We sugared off today," she wrote on the eighth and, again, on the 14th. "D. boiled sap all night, 200 pails full." At the time of this writing, both Keysars were 57 years of age. The spring of 1904 was a banner year. Following a sudden snowfall, which brought the sleighs out and "a great run-off sap," George collected a bountiful 900 pounds of the golden liquid.

With the relatively quiet winter months over, the Keysar farm became a place of energetic activity and the pace didn't appear to let up until the last hog was butchered in early December. Spring was a time for sawing wood (160 cord one year), "setting the geese" and horse and cattle trading. "Van Dyke is here to buy cattle," remarks Marinda in one entry. "Traded colts today," she notes in another, on April 23, 1890. On the 23rd, she cleans the cheese room; the 24th, finishes up sugaring and washes the buckets—all 200!

May was planting and sowing time (25 bushels of oats one year), a time for making soap and for welcoming newcomers to the farm. "Black Beauty (Marinda's prized black sow) has nine little pigs," she records proudly in May of 1899.

In June, they shear sheep. On July 4, 1890, the Keysars hold a family reunion with a picnic under the shade tree in the yard. July, as well as August, is also the heart of haying season. "D and Ben are helping (a neighbor) finish haying," she writes, on Aug. 15. (See note at end of chapter.) Marinda busies herself with making "31 (wheels of) cheese."

On Aug. 27, Marinda's three youngest children take the train to boarding school in Tilton and Westfield. She makes this slightly cryptic entry at the end of a school term in June 1894: "Children home, had old rooster for dinner."

On Sept. 8, Dudley serves as a juror in Colebrook Court. Harvesting begins, but Dudley takes time out for his annual trip to the Sherbrooke (Quebec) Fair. He begins digging potatoes on the 12th, with the threshers arriving on October 23. Marinda records a grand harvest of 535 bushels of oats in 1891.

It was also a time for fall cleaning and the household's move from the summer rooms into warmer quarters. In November, Marinda turns the farmhouse upside down, cleaning the pantry, taking up carpets and moving the stoves. On Dec. 4, "nearly all cleaned up. Made sausages today."

The Keysars, along with a large number of their family and neighbors, were members of the Advent Christian Church. They took time out of their busy lives to meet for worship, attending as many as three prayer meetings a week when traveling preachers visited the area.

On Nov. 18, 1901, Marinda loses her partner of 43 years. Rheumatic fever in 1892 apparently damaged his heart and this last year has been one of suffering for the 68-year-old farmer. His children take turns nursing him "night and day" through his last week of life. Her husband senses his end and, writes Marinda on November 16, "is so happy to think he is going." On Nov. 17, she writes," "O dear, we must part with him. Soon he has talked with all of us…. We are a sorrowful family." Dudley's heart gives out the following morning. "He died at half past one this morning. Can't be I am left alone," is Marinda's poignant entry.

Dudley Keysar started adult life as a clerk, his obituary observed, "but indoor life did not agree with him, so he bought a farm in Pittsburg where he spent the rest of his life, improving and adding to his farm until it has become one of the largest and best on Hall Stream." He followed in his father Benjamin's footsteps, the obituary continued, who had arrived in Stewartstown and Clarksville "when the country was new and thinly settled."

The Stewartstown-born man found a lifetime vocation, one he took great satisfaction in, as well he might. The 19th century was an era of self-sufficiency for the North Country. Farmers plowed and graded their own roads, nursed their sick and, with pantries and cellars filled with the results of their labor, had few reasons to turn to anyone for their daily needs.

Dudley found an able mate in Marinda Hart Keysar, who survived him by eight years. Several years after his death, she moved in with her daughter, Isabelle, and son-in-law Frank Perry, who had a farm in Canaan, Vermont. George, who had remained unmarried, continued to run the Keysar farm for five more years. Still, Marinda's heart remained where she had spent over 40 years of her life, at the farm "on the stream." When it was sold on May 2, 1906, Marinda made this single-line entry: "The home farm sold, $9,000." Above this line she adds this telling note, "A mistake."

Glenduen's childhood home once sat atop a crest on West Road in Clarksville. Glenduen Ladd collection.

The Dudley Keysar farm on Hall Stream in Pittsburg. Glenduen Ladd collection.

A classic scene, taken in 1910, at the Clarksville farm where Glenduen was born and raised. Glenduen Ladd photo.

Haying by hand. In 1927, farming was still largely done as it had been since the 1800s, as shown in this photo of haymakers that included Nelson Ladd (far left), and sons Fremont (third from left) and Harry (on wagon). Glenduen Ladd photo.

Glenduen's mother, Jennie, gathers peas into a wide bowl, perhaps in anticipation of preparing the northern New England "peas and potatoes" dish for the dinner table. (See recipe at end of chapter). Glenduen Ladd photo.

Harsh realities of farm life—an owl caught in trap near a hen coop on the Piper Hill farm in Stewartstown, taken in 1923. Glenduen Ladd photo.

The spotless condition of his prize cow and calf indicates that Canaan, Vermont, farmer Frank Perry (Marinda's son-in-law) may have been on his way to a country fair when he posed for this photo in 1908. Glenduen Ladd photo.

On August, 12, 1953, a reflective Frank Perry reclines where he had posed with his cows in 1908, at a farm later purchased by Glenduen and Harry. He had moved to Redlands, California, forty years earlier, where he grew oranges until the market bottomed out in the 1930s. He became a horse trainer, trading on a talent evidenced during his farming days in Canaan, where he had a reputation as a "horse whisperer." He could get a horse to do nearly anything, said one news clipping, showing a photo of a horse sitting on its haunches. Glenduen Ladd photo.

Mrs. Kelly poses on the horse-drawn hayer for her friends back home. Glenduen Ladd photo.

In 1939, Harry Ladd sharpens a farm implement with a grindstone, while paying guest Mr. Kelly looks on. The Ladds ran a guest house called "Broadlawn," on the corner of Route 102 and Canaan Hill Road (the former Frank Perry farm). Some chores on the Ladd farm continued to be done as they were in the early 1900s. Glenduen Ladd photo.

Marinda Keysar in 1919, near the end of a long life of labor. A clean white apron over her gingham floor length dress, her hair tightly drawn into a knot, hands folded on her lap, Marinda sits in a straight-back chair on the porch of her home, the years of toil written on her face. Glenduen Ladd photo.

Note: Haying for hours in the hot sun produced hefty appetites and workers looked forward to their noon dinner. The table was typically laden with such fare as peas and potatoes, cold sliced ham and fresh strawberries with ice cream and lemonade. Viola Sutton contributed this traditional farm recipe for peas and potato for the 1969 Bicentennial Edition of the Colebrook Cookbook: "1 quart of shelled green peas (or green beans), 7 to 8 new or small potatoes, 1/4 lb. Salt pork. Begin cooking salt pork (slit several times to rind) while preparing the vegetables. Add potatoes and cook until almost tender, then peas. (Do not overcook). Drain. Heat sufficient milk and cream (as rich as you like) real hot (under boiling point) and add to peas mixture. Salt and pepper to taste." (Viola notes that she believed this recipe had a French Canadian influence as it appeared to be unknown to people south of the Colebrook area.)

Chapter VI

HEARTH AND HOME

Keeping Up With
Farmer Jones

The American farmhouse may not have been equipped with the modern marvels of today's age, the microwave, dishwasher, electric stove and all the other trappings of 21st century life, but it was often a place of comfort and style. Woodstoves with elaborate nickel-plated fronts warmed the kitchen, intricately carved rocking chairs adorned nearly every room, beautifully patterned rugs brightened up wood and linoleum floors, rope portieres and lace curtains framed windows and nearly every parlor had a piano. By the early 20th century, plumbing had begun transforming the chamber pot from an item of necessity to one of decoration.

Glenduen also took great interest in interior decorating and all of her homes were beautifully arranged, as seen in this 1922 view of the front rooms of a home she owned next door to her in-laws on Piper Hill. The farm was later purchased by the Alex Guay family. Her last house was on Gale Street in Canaan, where she also took in guests. Glenduen Ladd photo.

In 1911, Glenduen's father, Horace Wells, relaxes with his newspaper near the warmth of the nickel-plated, embossed woodstove in his Clarksville farmhouse. The kitchen was the place to gather at the end of a long day of work. Glenduen Ladd photo.

State-of-the-art bathroom at Glenduen's Piper Hill home in the late 1920s, with marble counter, gilded mirror, hook for the razor strop and a spacious linen closet. Glenduen Ladd photo.

Framed by an arch of ivy, rocking chairs beckon invitingly on the front porch of Glenduen's "Broadlawn" tourist home in Canaan, Vermont. The front porch was another favorite gathering place in the early 1900s, and remained so even in 1940, when this photo was taken. Glenduen Ladd photo.

Chapter VII

"THE CHURCH ON THE STREAM"

Advent Christians and the Millerites

Marinda Keysar made an entry in her journal on June 10, 1883, recording a significant event in North Country history. "The men here have gone to help raise the A.C. (Advent Christian) church," Marinda wrote.

Marinda was a devout Advent Christian, along with all her family and a large number of people living in the region. Many of Marinda's observations made during the 17 years she kept a journal revolved around the religious activities in her area. It puts a personal face on the history of a religious denomination that, before the close of the 19th century, had become one of the major religions in northern New England and the eastern townships of Canada.

The church Marinda was referring to was built on what is now Hall Stream Road in Hereford, Quebec. L.C. Channell's History of Compton County, written in 1896, contains a chapter on the township of Hereford. It fills some of the gaps left by Marinda. "At Hall's Stream, there is an Advent Christian church, with D.W. Davis as pastor," wrote Channell. "At

Hall's Stream, Adventist teachings were first introduced nearly forty years ago, by A. Gordon, and have been advocated at times by others since then. Some ten years ago, there was a church organized by seven members, with C.O. Hibbard as elder and D. Keysar and H. Nichols as deacons. Since then accessions have been made until there are now over thirty-five members. In 1892 a neat and commodious church was erected. It is now in a fairly prosperous condition, with average attendance of about seventy-five."

A discrepancy between Channell's book and Marinda's journal exists as to the date that the church was built, but Channell's research does identify the Keysars as being charter members of the Hall Stream Advent Christian Church, a fact also included in Marinda's obituary. D. (Dudley) Keysar, Marinda's husband, is named as one of the original deacons.

According to Marinda's journal, the first meeting in the new church was conducted by "Elder" Whitman on October 21, 1883. On Oct. 22, she writes, "Dedication sermon at 2. The house was packed to its utmost and everything passed off pleasantly." She mentions D.W. Davis in her journal, recording that he left as pastor in 1896.

The 1891 census in Hereford showed a total of 98 people claiming the Adventist faith as their own, making it the third largest denomination in Hereford. That figure indicates the growth in the north of this religious organization, which had sprung from the Millerite movement of the mid-nineteenth century.

William Miller, a longtime Vermont resident, served as an army officer in the War of 1812. Although having been a skeptic at one point in his adult life, Miller later embarked on a study of the books of Daniel and Revelation. He came to the conclusion that Jesus Christ's Second Coming or Advent, accompanied by the end of the world and the ascension to heaven of the faithful, would occur sometime between March 21, 1843 and March 21, 1844. That would mark the start of Christ's millennial (thousand year) reign.

Miller garnered a huge following, which, at the movement's peak, numbered abut 50,000. The dates he set came and went without the expected events taking place, leading to what the Adventists call "The Great Disappointment." Many people abandoned their belief in the imminent coming of Christ. However, others still held that Christ's advent was near. Several Adventist bodies emerged out of Miller's evangelism, including the Advent Christian Church, which was officially formed in 1860.

Advent Christians continued to believe they were living in the "last days." They emphasized the importance of obeying Jesus' commission at Matthew 24:14, "This gospel of the kingdom shall be preached in all the world for a witness unto all the nations and then the end shall come," according to the 1899 Advent Christian publication, **The Leadings Of God**. This publication, written by Josephine Lawson, showed that some members took up mission work, traveling to cities and towns and distributing tracts in the streets and from door to door. Josephine's missions took her to the eastern townships of Quebec and the villages of northern New Hampshire, including stays in Alton Bay, Franconia and Littleton.

Marinda and Dudley often housed and fed itinerate or traveling preachers, including Elder Gordon who was mentioned in Channell's book. Very little deterred these devout people from attending their religious services and they traveled in winter by sleigh over the bridge from Pittsburg into Hereford. The Keysars attended the prayer and tent meetings held when traveling preachers were in the area.

Marinda mentions attending a tent meeting in Clarksville on June 5, 1898. This was probably held in the field across from the old Clarksville Schoolhouse where the **Colebrook Chronicle** and **Lancaster Herald** are now published. The field now contains a sign proclaiming the spot to be the 45th parallel, the halfway point between "the North Pole and the Equator". Everett Wiswell, born about 1889, gives his own perspective of the tent meetings held in Clarksville in his book, **King Phillip's Territory**. "In the 1890's, a group of people in the central part of the state started sending missionaries up to convert these heatherns [sic] up here. They came with a tent which they pitched on Keysar flat opposite Stewart Batchelder's now, at the foot of North Hill and beside Clarksville Pond Brook which was dammed up for a place to wash sins away."

The Keysars visited their neighbors, soliciting funds for their church and stocking firewood for the church stove—a task which had its difficulties. "D. went with a load of wood to church and tipped over and hurt his ankle quite badly," wrote Marinda on January 31, 1895.

Even during the last years of Marinda's life, when she was crippled with rheumatism, she attended church in what she called her "wheeled chair." Her obituary published in the Advent Christian Church publication entitled **The World**

Crisis acknowledged her dedication with these words, "Mrs. Keysar…was never absent from its services until ill health compelled her to give up what to her was one of the pleasantest things of life, meeting for worship in God's house." Her funeral, conducted by C.W. Shattuck, was held on April 9, 1910, at the "church on the stream" that she had helped establish. Glenduen noted the passing of Elder Shattuck in 1951, at a nursing home in Center Harbor, and clipped out his obituary for her scrapbook.

Pasted into Marinda's journal are several clippings, including obituaries and sermons, from **The World Crisis**, published by Warren Press in Boston. "The Advent movement was a very literate movement," said Louis Going, pastor of the Advent Christian Church in Whitefield, during a 2002 interview with this author. Horace Lorenzo Hastings, one of its key leaders, said Pastor Going, had been involved with Miller and was "very influential in terms of printing. The printing was prolific." Many of these theological materials, including **The World Crisis**, were printed on the Advent press on Warren Street in Boston.

The obituaries revealed almost as much about Adventist beliefs as the sermons. "Now she sleeps well, awaiting the call of Him who hath been her God through life and will guard sacredly the sleeping dust until the morning," reads Marinda's obituary.

These comments and many similar ones in other Adventist obituaries, reveal the Adventist belief that the soul was the entire person, mind and body, not a separate entity that separated from the body at death. Upon death, a loved one was believed to be unconscious, "sleeping" in the grave until the Christ's Second Coming and the resurrection of that person back to an earth free from pain, sickness and death. That ideology is where the Adventists departed from Miller's teachings. "Miller didn't hold to the 'sleep of the soul,' said Pastor Going.

Glenduen grew up attending the Hall Stream church. Her husband's parents, Nelson and Grace Ladd, who had a farm on Piper Hill in Stewartstown, were also members at one point, as revealed in letters kept by Grace spanning over half a century.

A letter from Albert Gordon (no doubt the same A. Gordon mentioned by Channell), written from Richmond, Vermont in 1898, begins with the salutation, "Dear Brethren and Sisters in Christ…I often think of bygone days when we used to meet together to worship God. O how I should like the privilege again…be assured I have not forgotten the little band."

A letter from Elder Charles Clark addresses Grace and Nelson as "Bro. and Sister Ladd." He also asks to be remembered to Grace's parents, "Brother (Osman) and Sister (Susan) Forrest, and to Susan's spinster sibling, "Sister Fidelia," who lived with her sister's family at the Ladd farm. Several years later, in 1908, it was Clark's sad duty to conduct the funeral service held for "Brother Ivo," Grace and Nelson's 21-year-old son, who died from injuries resulting in a kick from a horse at Tom Van Dyke's lumber camp in Hereford.

Following Ivo's death, condolences poured in from relatives far and wide, which revealed that many of the extended Ladd family had an Adventist background, including the publisher of Laconia's **News and Critic**, Albert M. Weeks, Grace's cousin. His mother, Laurinda (Hilliard) Weeks, was one of 12 children, of whom at least four others—Sara, Persis, Fidelia and Susan (Grace's mother)—were Adventists.

The Advent Christian Church on Hall Stream was eventually moved closer to the border and is now a residence. With the passing of the original church members and the ebbing of the Adventist movement in the North Country, the younger generation was absorbed into area denominations. Marinda's daughter Jennie became a Congregationalist and Glenduen later became a member of the Grace United Methodist Church in Canaan, Vermont.

Some Adventist church buildings were later used as community churches, such as the Advent church in Kidderville, a tight-knit farming section of Colebrook. For many years, that building housed a Congregationalist congregation, but it fell into disuse during the 1980s. It was torn down on December 30, 2002, following a ecumenical deconsecrating ceremony by area clergy.

Today, Advent Christians number about 40,000 in the United States. The northernmost Advent congregation in New Hampshire is in Whitefield, housed in the oldest structure in town. In 1999, the Whitefield congregation celebrated the church's 150th anniversary.

The church is likely the Christian Advent Church on Hall Stream in Hereford. Glenduen (with hat) and Harry stand next to Harry's father Nelson Ladd (circa 1920). The church was later moved from its location next to the Advent cemetery. It is now a residence, fourth house on the left after crossing U.S. Customs, according to cemetery trustee Cheryl Clogston. Glenduen Ladd collection.

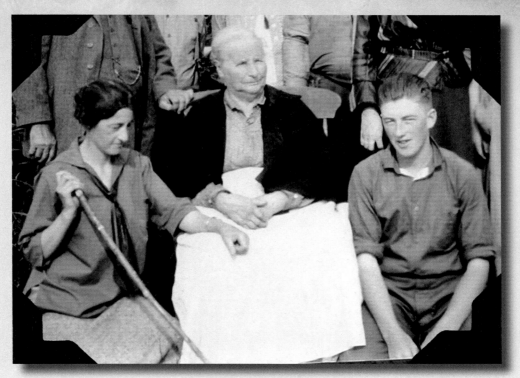

Fidelia Hilliard, last surviving member of 12 children, most of whom had belonged to the Advent Christian religion. A spinster, she lived out her days on the Piper Hill farm of her sister Susan's daughter, Grace Ladd. She was known for her strong religious faith and devotion to reading the Bible. Glenduan Ladd collection.

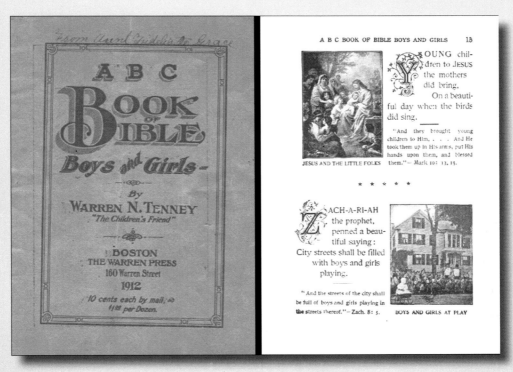

Left, learning the ABCs the Bible way. "From Aunt Fidelia to Grace" wrote Fidelia, across the top of an Advent Christian children's reader that she presented to her young niece, Grace Carbee; right, the letter Z features Bible writer Zachariah's words, "boys and girls at play," in a scene more representative of small town America than the Biblical Middle East. Author's collection.

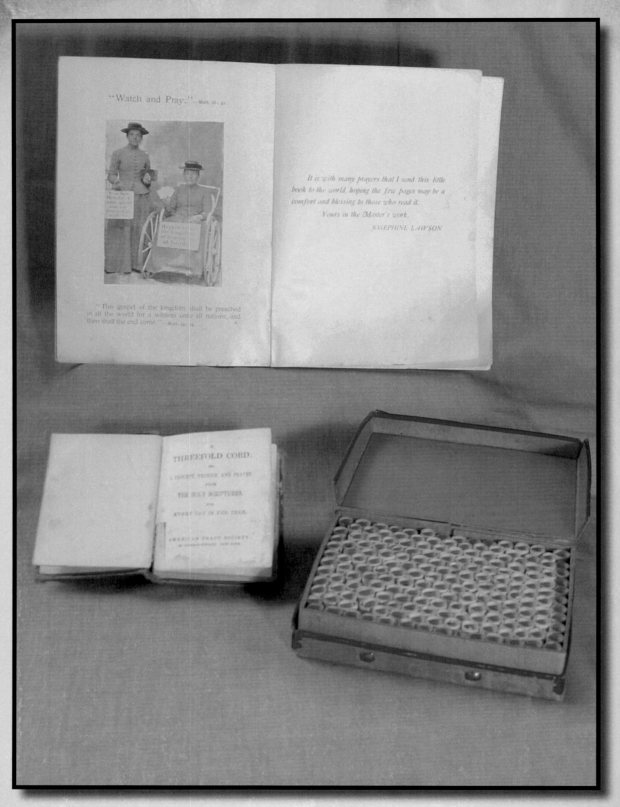

Adventist material found in Grace Ladd's trunk included The Leadings Of God, published by the Advent Christian Publication Society in Boston, depicting author Josephine Lawson (in wheelchair) and Mary H. Winslow in tract work; A Threefold Cord, by the American Tract Society in New York (with daily scriptural texts); and a box with scripture texts written on tiny paper scrolls. The box cover had this inscription, "Thy words were found, and I did eat them." Jer.15. 16. Susan Zizza photo.

Jennie Wells, Marinda and Dudley's daughter, on her way to church (circa 1920). Glenduen Ladd photo.

Chapter VIII

HOMESTEADERS OF HEREFORD

The Nest Egg of a Revolutionary War Soldier

Standing like a sentinel in the front row of the Old Hall Stream Cemetery in East Hereford is one of the oldest gravestones in this eastern provincial township of Quebec.

Carved into the thin grayish-green slate are the name of New Hampshire native Ezekiel Flanders and a bare-bones history of his life on this earth—including his date of birth in 1761 and his death in 1846. What makes this burial plot unusual is that it is the final resting place of an American Revolutionary War veteran. He is surrounded largely by headstones dating from the mid-19th to the mid-20th century.

The answer as to how a soldier of George Washington's Continental Army came to be buried on what was then British soil lies in documents recorded by Glenduen Ladd and filed with the cemetery's trustees. Those records also tell of the cemetery restoration project led by Glenduen and supported by East Hereford residents, along with descendants of the cemetery's occupants.

In August 1956, Glenduen set in motion the restoration of the cemetery, which included the burial plots of her great-grandparents, Hiram Sr., and Lavina (Colby) Wells. The earliest grave is that of an infant, who died in 1831, at the age of two months. Years of neglect had resulted in the headstones' near-obliteration by trees, brush and sod. Glenduen began a writing campaign, composing hundreds of letters to those who had family buried there, in order to raise funds and gain support. The thoroughness of Glenduen's letter campaign is indicated by the fact that she elicited funds from as far away as Michigan, where Ezekiel's son, Francis, eventually settled. Throughout the project, Glenduen took photographs, preserving images of what the cemetery looked like before the work commenced, the work in progress and the end result. She also drew a detailed map of the lots and recorded all the information she could find on those buried there. She recorded every gift of money, labor and resources given to the cemetery. This document is about 60 pages in length.

Identification of grave sites was not an easy task. "Some of the stones were two to three feet under the ground," said Glenduen's niece, Beverly Uran. Beverly went with her aunt to work on the cemetery nearly every week day." We went through the cemetery with a testing iron, through every inch of ground, pushing through till we heard metal on stone."

Once the stones were found, according to Beverly, the men shoveled up the stones, pulled them out and laid them in the sun to dry. "They were crumbling to the touch, very soft, like a salt lick. The sun dried them out and they hardened. Then we would scrub them with Comet and bleach and repair the broken stones."

Beverly can remember crawling through the brush on hands and knees, cutting with clippers and scythes. It was hard work, with some startling moments, including the time she came suddenly upon a skull—which turned out to be, not human, but that of a long-deceased cow.

Old Hall Stream Cemetery trustee Cheryl Clogston, whose mother, Gertrude Owen, was also a trustee, has similar memories. She recalled how many of the town's youngsters worked on the project with their parents. "We carried brush, scrubbed stones, we all pitched in." The project was completed in October 1958, and an endowment of several thousand dollars was set up to help maintain the cemetery.

The inhabitants of the old cemetery represent a cross-section of the varied background of this area's settlers. According to the **Townships Heritage WebMagazine**, produced by the Townshippers' Association, the earliest settlement in the land now known as the Eastern Townships began in the 17th century with the Abenakis. Place names such as Coaticook, Magog, and Memphremagog reflect that history. So does the gravestone of a descendant of those very early settlers, Mary Titus, an Abenaki raised by a white family on Titus Hill in Colebrook.

Mary and her husband, David Hodge, moved to Hereford Hill after settling Hodge Valley in Dixville Notch. Her great-grandson, Neil Tillotson (owner of the Balsams Grand Resort until his death in 2001, at the age of 102), was born on Hereford Hill in 1898, later becoming the inventor of a phenomenally successful rubber patent. He founded Tillotson Corporation and built a manufacturing plant in Hodge Valley in Dixville Notch, where his grandparents had homesteaded. This ingenious entrepreneur also worked with Glenduen (his cousin) on the cemetery restoration project, funding, among other things, a gate and fence. The Tillotson Foundation continues to provide funds to help maintain the Old Hall Stream Cemetery.

Some of the wives' names on headstones hint of French heritage, but all the surnames in the old cemetery are English. During the French regime, southern Quebec remained without a survey, with French settlers preferring to stick close to the St. Lawrence River.

In 1792, the British opened this remote part of Canada to settlement and set up the township system. Instead of dividing land into "seigneuries" granted to feudal lords, the British divided land into townships, 10 miles by 10 miles, which would be granted to "leaders." The township would be divided up into lots of 200 acres, which the leader would grant to settlers called "associates."

Some Loyalists fleeing the United States during the American Revolution were offered grants. It has been said that the first white settlers of the Eastern Townships were Loyalists, but they were few in number and settlement in the harsh wilderness of the southern border was slow. It has also been said that development was hindered more by corruption and speculation than by the area's climate and remoteness. By 1838, of 100 landowners holding 1,500,000 acres in the Eastern Townships, only six actually resided there.

The vast majority of the early pioneers, states the Townshippers Association's history, were not Loyalists, but hardy American pioneers looking for "good, cheap land and opportunity." There was a large influx of American immigrants from the late 1790s, continuing into the 1820s. Among them were Kingston (New Hampshire)-born Ezekiel Flanders, his wife Betsy and son Francis.

Cheap land, even land belonging to the British Crown he had just been liberated from, may have looked pretty good to Ezekiel Flanders. The paper money issued by Congress, according to the book, **The Boys of '76,** was "poor stuff. It was only a promise to pay and the promise was not worth much." It took 100 Continental dollars to buy one pair of boots; 500 of those dollars to buy a good coat.

From the time of his enlistment at Plaistow, New Hampshire, in 1777, Ezekiel served in several regiments, including those stationed at Saratoga and West Point, New York. He left West Point within the month that Benedict Arnold's attempted betrayal of the Hudson River fort's position was foiled and a planned British invasion averted.

Ezekiel, by now a sergeant, was discharged by General Washington in June 1783, shortly before the Paris treaty in September, when the United States was recognized as a free and independent nation. He rejoined the army briefly to fill out another soldier's term, receiving his final discharge in the spring of 1784.

An 1833 deposition given by Flanders, in connection with his pension request, reveals that he had been in Hereford since at least 1813, according to cemetery records. Although his son was born in Sutton, New Hampshire, in 1792, Flanders may well have left for township territory shortly after his son's birth. By 1832, land was still only "four shillings an acre," according to the **Emigrant's Directory and Guide,** written by the Eastern Townships land agent, Francis Evans, that same year.

It is interesting to note that Ezekiel didn't apply for his pension until the age of 72, perhaps because of lingering doubts about the relatively new U.S. government's ability to produce it. For his future, Ezekiel made arrangements to give 50 acres "in the 4th Range of Hereford" to Glenduen's great-grandfather. Hiram Wells was to maintain a small farm for Ezekiel and Betsy's sustenance, provide the aging couple with "comfortable accommodations," a good supply of wood and a small plot for a garden.

This type of arrangement was a common method of obtaining land under Crown law. "Persons advanced in life…desire to make their old age comfortable with labor," wrote land agent Evans. "They will give their farms, implements and stock to an honest industrious person, who binds himself either to support them during their lives or else may pay them for a certain rent for the same term."

Thus, the land of a British king became an American Revolutionary veteran's retirement nest egg.

A post card, circa 1900, of Hereford at the Hereford Hill turn, near the former site of the Advent Christian church and the pioneer cemetery restored by Glenduen and other descendants of the early settlers. Glenduen Ladd collection.

A work crew at the Old Hall Stream Cemetery on July 2, 1957, in Hereford, Quebec. Far right, Beverly (Hunt) Uran. Others in the photo may be Ray and Fay Wells and Charlie Gray, who contributed much time, labor and resources to restoring the cemetery. Glenduen Ladd photo, courtesy Old Hall Stream Cemetery trustees.

Glenduen Ladd with a fellow worker on a cool July day in 1957. Photo courtesy Old Hall Stream Cemetery trustees.

Hereford's pioneer cemetery at the onset of the restoration project in 1956. Glenduen Ladd photo, courtesy Old Hall Stream Cemetery trustees.

In 1960, standing in straight, neatly mowed rows, enhanced by blooming plants, the cleaned and repaired headstones were unrecognizable from their previous state. Glenduen Ladd photo, courtesy Old Hall Stream Cemetery trustees.

Industrialist and inventor Neil Tillotson, who, for 40 years was first in the nation to vote in the presidential election, collaborated with his cousin, Glenduen, in the restoration project. On May 8, 2001, at 102 years of age, he reminisced at his Dixville office about his accomplished contemporary. "I went to her beautiful home on Gale Street every Christmas. She reminded me of the girls I went to school with, a lady. She really had put her heart into that (cemetery project)." Susan Zizza photo.

Chapter IX

THE WILD, WILD NORTH

"A Trek with the Tramp"

The settlements in the narrow valleys of northern New England were still ringed with deep forests and wild terrain at the turn of the century and were the domain of hardy frontiersmen, including Nelson Ladd and his sons Harry and Ivo. Nelson was born on January 12, 1854, in Stewartstown, where, except for a short period, he lived all of his life. He died at his farm on Piper Hill on March 12, 1937, at the age of 83.

His passing merited headlines in the pages of Laconia's **News and Critic**. "Nelson I. Ladd Dies in Stewartstown, Widely Known Hunter and Guide," writes J. Fremont Weeks. "His life-story embraces much of the early history of his town and vicinity from the days when Indians ranged the forests or followed the trail from Canada leading through Dixville Notch to Maine, when his immediate forbears related tales of the last chief, Metalak, who due to blindness passed his remaining days with the whites. Log cabins had scarcely been replaced with comfortable homes when 'Nel' Ladd was

born in the neighborhood of Stewartstown Hollow. One of his thrilling anecdotes was that of being chased by a bear one night on his return home from a distant neighbor's house."

Letters to his sweetheart (Sarah) Grace Forrest, later to become his wife, reveal that Nelson was an adventurer, but he preferred his adventures close to home. Before his marriage in 1884, he had traveled to Colorado to seek work, but was unimpressed with the Wild West. He wrote to teenaged Grace that he had traveled "about fore thousand miles since I left home and have seen all I want to." He returned east and began working as a "driver of buckboard conveyances at hotel resorts of the White Mountains," according to Week's article, including Fabyan House in Crawford Notch. Again, his letters from Crawford Notch were homesick dispatches expressing his longing for his home in the Colebrook area.

Nelson was a crack shot, writes Weeks. "The lore of the woods really became his ruling passion as a subject of study in his early manhood which qualified him to be one of the best shots in the region and won for him many trophies at Thanksgiving turkey shoots or in any contests where expert marksmanship counted. He knew his way far and wide in the woodlands particularly in the resorts of fish and game and he seldom returned from the hunt without his quota of game, the surplus of which was always shared with his own and neighboring families. This trait combined with his genial nature and goodfellowship made him the soul of the camp in forest or stream as those who have enjoyed his company on such occasions will ever attest."

A **News and Critic** columnist, who wrote under the *nom de plume* of "The Tramp," gave the following firsthand account of a hunting trip to Millsfield Pond Brook in Dixville Notch with a camping party that included Nelson, Harry and Ivo Ladd, written before Ivo's untimely death in 1908.

"The party of eight, who left Colebrook Wednesday morning, June 11, embraced in its personnel some of the most renowned woodsmen of the upper Coos region. It was headed by "Nell" Ladd and his two sons, Harry and Ivo, all of them inbred frontiersmen and familiar with every inch of the country to which our matched team of dappled grey roadsters were taking us with camp and equipage. Then there was "Bill" Stillings, always on hand at the dinner hour, and last but not least, Irving Little, 'chip of the old block fisherman,' who most always came home with a basketful. The drive of twenty miles up the Mohawk river took us through Dixville notch to our camping place seven miles beyond, on the shore of Millsfield pond brook near its junction with Clear stream. Here we pitched our tent, and by the time the vanguard of the party in the second team arrived, luncheon was ready. It was served in true camper's style, with hot coffee done to a flavor that will make the homemade article insipid to the taste for many weeks to come, to those who filled their cups from the kettle urn which hung over the camp fire.

Fishing for brook trout began almost as soon as we arrived in camp, some of the boys trying their lines in the stream nearby. After dinner the fun began in earnest and notwithstanding the high water the first afternoon, fishing was attended with good success. During the three days in camp, the sport was carried on with a zest and most of the numerous tributaries of Clear stream were gone over. Some of the party tried their luck on Millsfield pond with good success. Clear stream drains the slope and empties into the Androscoggin at Errol. The Dixville mountains and those of Wentworth's Location, divide the slope watered by Clear stream from that of the Swift Diamond valley and is undoubtedly the best fishing and hunting region in this part of the north country.

The water was considered too high for brook trout fishing as when the streams reach in lower water line the speckled beauties are found grouped together in the large pools and accordingly possess a sharper appetite having less territory in which to satisfy in. However, our party secured about 40 lbs. of dressed trout during the three days' fishing which was quite good luck. Beginning as a novice, I was more than pleased by my success and flatter myself that I have acquired a little knowledge of the fascinating art in the limited time I had to practice. It was also worth something to me to visit a country like that described,—"Where rolls the Oregon, that hears no sound save its own dashing." For just east of our camp began the rugged outline of Wentworths Location and extended a country where perhaps you might wander three hundred miles in an almost interminable forest. But I have not any real big fish stories to tell, the lakes and ponds of this country are where you get those, in fact most everybody was trying their luck at fly fishing up there and fat catches on "Big Diamond," Leach and Greenough ponds were reported. The biggest one I saw was caught by Harry Chamberlain of West Stewartstown on Leach, which came near being a three-pounder. Fred Vancore of Colebrook, also caught a big string on Big Diamond, 16 of them tipping the scales at 22 pounds. Greenough pond in Errol is particularly mentioned as a good fishing resort. Here, George Demerritt has a sporting camp, terms $1.50 per day, and to hook a trout weighing from one to four pounds is a common occurrence. The place is in close proximity to Little Greenough and Bear Brook pond and better fishing is claimed for the quality than for some of the more noted resorts.

Our party was particularly fortunate in having as a member the noted river man and guide, Nelson I. Ladd of Colebrook. Besides being a crack fisherman, he has won laurels in the hunting arena and there is little territory in northern New Hampshire and Maine that he is not familiar with. The last day in camp we took a tramp up the "tote" road" several miles to fish down the Corser brook. On the way we got a glimpse of a deer in his native heath. He was in easy gun shot range, but quickly shipped his flag to the breeze and was out of sight in an instant. He was a fine specimen…

…As I have said, we passed through Dixville Notch, and as some one has said in Sweetser's White Mountain: 'It is one of the wildest and most imposing pieces of rock and mountain scenery on the Atlantic side of our country. Totally different from, and therefore not to be compared with, any of the passes among the White Mountains, it has peculiar characteristics, which are not equaled elsewhere. In general it may be said that the Notch looks as if it had been produced by a convulsion of nature, which broke the mountain ridge from underneath, throwing the strata of rocks up into the air, and letting them fall in all directions. The Profile is seen from a guide-board on the right of the road, high up on the cliffs and is preferred by some visitors to the Franconia Profile, on account of its variety of expressions.'

A new road of even grade through the notch is now nearly completed for which the last legislature made an appropriation of $3000. This was increased to three times that sum by Messr. Hale and son of Philadelphia, the new proprietors of the Dix house at the notch. The hotel and grounds have been very much improved and an artificial fish pond constructed. The Hales have also secured a large tract of the adjacent country and are improving the same for agricultural purposes as evidenced by the splendid barn and cupola which we saw as we drove by. The region has been re-christened "The Balsams," and it is evident that the proprietors intend to secure for their friends and patrons a natural hunting and fishing park. They have recently purchased lands on Millsfield pond, near where we camped, this they have named "Lake Gloriette." Here they have constructed a hunting lodge and are now building a carriage road to the same along the Millsfield stream.

In closing this sketch, I will just mention my visit at the State Fish Hatchery at Colebrook. It is one of the largest in the state and secured through the influence of J.H. Dudley, Esq., of Colebrook, some ten years ago when he was in the senate. A.C. Wallace, the superintendent in charge, has been connected with the hatchery from the start and courteously showed me about the premises. Last year, a large fish pond was constructed and a new building 32x50 feet built, with capacity for hatching two and one half million frye. Eight hundred thousand have been this season distributed in the waters of the Upper Coos region in about every town and as far south as Haverhill on the Boston and Maine railroad, and Lower Bartlett on the Maine Central. Mr. Wallace gave me the figures, but space prevents printing the list of distribution. The pond swarmed with brook trout kept for breeding purposes and the twenty-eight hatching troughs were alive with little fellows just out of the sack stage. The trout are fed ground liver, which requires an order of two or three hundred pounds a week, from the city of Portland, to make sure of a supply. THE TRAMP."

Writer J. Fremont Weeks describes a later hunting trip with Nelson, his son Harry and Nelson's son-in-law Harold Carbee, who later became Colebrook's chief of police:

"J.F. Weeks of this paper returned Monday afternoon from a week's stay in the Dixville Notch region after the festive deer, and as a result of his expedition, brought home with him a handsome ten-point buck. He was the guest of Nelson I. Ladd and party of Stewartstown, who is one of the most expert deer hunters of the north country. Mr. Ladd met the writer at the train with his fine pair of black horses, and the party arrived at "Spruce Bluff Camp," a few miles out beyond the Notch, in time for supper, and everything was ready to begin the five-days' hunt at the first streak of dawn the next day. It is not necessary to describe the incidents in detail, only to say that it was one of the most successful and enjoyable of any within the writer's several years of experience at this ideal hunting resort. All kinds of game was in the woods, but wary, and it required the utmost exertion of all the skill of these noted Nimrods, not to mention the one of less repute.

Having in a general way referred to the senior members of the party, especial mention should be given to "the boys." first in war and first at the table was Harold Carbee, a good fellow of course, but extremely versatile in his makeup. A good deer hunter, too, and has all the big game hunters beaten to a frazzle as a guide. He can tread the pathless forest or shin up a tree to get the lay of the land, in the darkest night and can play tag around a tree with an infuriated deer at the fastest possible pace. Then he has particular talent as an actor—ask Harry. You bet he is a humorist! He kept the campers in uproarious merriment most of the time. The writer forswears to say more on this line, for he was warned not to mention him in that—er—News and Critic.

Harry Ladd was quite as good as an impersonator. The writer has heretofore been inclined to characterize him as "Hurry Harry," he being a good representation of this fictitious personage in Cooper's "Leather Stocking Tales," but he was the emblem of patience on this occasion and alert enough to locate a 200-pound buck on a high bluff by the west side of the opening and brought him down with his self loading Remington, with a finishing pill from his Colt's double-action revolver. His specialty in the camp was buying and selling credulous humanity. He didn't dare to do it when he made biscuit, for rocks were not handy and hard articles in the bread line would have been at a premium.

Clyde Parker Hall, the kid of the party, could see a deer under every bush. He even talked of them in his sleep. It was agreed by all the wakeful ones at night to awaken him when he began talking, lest he inadvertently reveal some of his "dear" escapades. He is some hunter, just the same, and always gets his two ere the season closes."

Guide Nelson Ladd and two companions head to Nathan Pond in the wilds of Dixville, on a June 9-13, 1914, fishing trip. Festooned with rolled bedding, hand-woven fishing creels and fishing rods and gear tucked away in carrying cases, the trio look prepared for all exigencies, especially the gentleman with holstered gun on hip. (Karen DeFelice of Lakeshore Crafts in Pittsburg weaves fishing baskets patterned after the old-fashioned style of those shown in the photo.) Glenduen Ladd photo.

At a woods camp in 1912, Nelson Ladd with son-in-law Harold Carbee (to left) and newspaperman J. Fremont Weeks of the Laconia News and Critic (second to right), along with other hunting cronies. Glenduen Ladd photo.

Guide Nelson Ladd displays his catch. Glenduen Ladd photo.

Gladys Green, at an Averill Lake outing in 1929, with her catch of the day. The fairer sex apparently had no need to trek deep into the wilderness to put supper on the table! Glenduen Ladd photo.

Chapter X

HAVING THE LAST WORD

Obituaries—Honesty in the Press

If it weren't for the obituaries frankly written and carefully preserved, little would have been known about those who formed the foundation of the North Country—Chief Justice Robert Chamberlain, newspaper editor Alma Cummings, stage coach driver Hiram Blanchard, lumber baron George Van Dyke and centenarian Elizabeth Kidder, an early settler who remembered the day George Washington died.

These and many more are the historical figures who enliven the pages of a scrapbook filled with almost seven decades of newspaper clippings. The scrapbook was found in the attic of Nelson Ladd's 19th century Piper Hill farmhouse, among letters and mementos belonging to his wife, Grace. Grace was born in 1865 and died in 1945, just a few months before the end of World War II.

By compiling the recorded exit of family, neighbors and acquaintances from life's stage, this kitchen table historian left a window wide open into the past, affording posterity a glimpse of history far more intimate and moving than any dry tome on a library shelf.

Grace, as she was called, was born in Jefferson, New Hampshire, but lived on her grandfather's farm at the foot of Piper Hill in Stewartstown until she was five years old. In 1870, she, along with her parents, Osmond and Susan Forrest, moved into a farmhouse at the top of Piper Hill, where she was to spend the rest of her life.

For most of those years, Grace collected newspaper clippings, a hodgepodge of literally hundreds of obituaries, news items, sermons, poems and household hints. She pasted them over samples of penmanship and lines of ciphers in an old school composition book and filled a box with the overflow.

The oldest clipping dates from 1878, which notes the passing of "Miss Polly Blodgett, aged 74 years," a spinster who devoted her life to an invalid sister and her brother's orphaned children. The last obituary, dated 1936, is that of Grace's cousin, Albert M. Weeks of Weeks Brothers, publishers of the **News and Critic** in Laconia.

Life on a homestead which had barely been wrested from the forest was not easy. Many of Grace's early clippings show that the young wife and mother felt a kinship with the early settlers who endured great hardship in order to carve out homes in this northern wilderness.

Centenarian Elizabeth Kidder arrived in Stewartstown in 1822. "The old lady remembered very vividly (a few weeks before her death in the early 1890s) the time when George Washington died," reads her obituary, "and she has told the writer that it was a very dark day when they got the news of this death…her father won laurels in the war of 1776 at Saratoga and West Point… Times were not as they are now. The log cabin was her palace and the hand loom her throne. Cooking stoves were then unknown. Meetings were held in kitchens, schoolhouses and barns… In 1837, she was led down into the water and received baptism…She thought that ministers and Christians had changed very much since the time she was a girl."

Dolly Brainard Aldrich's obituary begins, "Another of the old settlers in this north country passed away." Born in 1832, Dolly was the daughter of Lucy Beecher, cousin to renowned theologian and abolitionist Henry Ward Beecher, whose sister, Harriet Beecher Stowe, authored **Uncle Tom's Cabin**. "….Lucy Beecher would tell of the time," the obituary continued, "when they rode on horse back, mother and daughter, a child of four, all the way to Stewartstown (from Connecticut) on one horse."

Hiram Blanchard of Pittsburg merited attention, both as a "genial, cheery man," and as a stage coach driver on the Stratford to Colebrook run for two decades. He was also Deputy Collector of Customs under "Cleveland's last administration."

Benjamin Buel Jordan's contributions to the region are recorded, including his participation in building of the first dam across the Androscoggin at Errol. The obituary of this lifelong bachelor reads, "While he could not boast of doing great things, it can truthfully be said of him that he did many good things." In 1926, Colebrook's last member of the Grand Army of the Republic, Alfred Newton Alls, died at the age of 84. "Alfred's parents came to Columbia to live, where he attended the log cabin school house," reads his obituary. He responded to President Abraham Lincoln's call for volunteers and was mustered into Company I of the Heavy Artillery, which guarded the nation's capitol.

Another alumnus of North Country schools was Chief Justice Robert N. Chamberlain of the Superior Court of New Hampshire, who died at the age of 61, following an operation. He attended schools in West Stewartstown and Colebrook, worked in a private office in Canaan, Vermont, and began active practice in 1881. He was Speaker of the House of Representatives and was on Governor Jordan's staff.

Another mover and shaker in New England's wooded north was the man known as the "Lumber King of the Connecticut Valley." That was George Van Dyke, born on Feb. 21, 1846, in Stanbridge, Quebec. The obituary details the auto accident that took the life of Van Dyke and his 30-year-old chauffeur, Fred B. Hodgdon of Lancaster. "It is supposed the driver took hold of the wrong lever," relates the writer, as the car rested on the edge of a 75-foot drop along the Connecticut River in Riverside, Massachusetts. "In a second it was over the rock precipice…Mr. VanDyke with characteristic energy jumped from the machine in an effort to save himself from going over the bank. The machine turned completely over and buried the driver Mr. Hodgden underneath, Mr. VanDyke falling on the rocks 20 feet away. He was a very heavy man and it was only with great difficulty that the river men were able to get his body to more level ground." Van Dyke was taken to a nearby hospital, where he died several hours later. The writer goes on to describe the lumber baron's early beginnings. "He was what you call a self-made man. He secured his only education from a four years attendance at a country school, and when 11 years old began to earn his own living, going into the woods and chopping all day and taking his earnings home to his mother at night. Without a cent of capital, or an influential backer, with nothing but his rugged strength and his quick wit, he made himself the richest and most powerful lumberman in New England."

Gad Beecher's obituary states that he "figured prominently in the early industries of (Stewartstown) and at one time operated a woolen factory near the present site of Parker's Shop… and furnished valuable services in starting the **Frontier Gazette**, about twenty years ago, having secured over 300 subscribers before the first issue made its appearance." Gad was the son of Marcus Beecher, "an old Revolutionary pensioner who came here in 1802 from Connecticut and first settled at the Narrows."

Gad, taken from the name of the Biblical patriarch Jacob's son, isn't a name commonly heard when attendance is taken in school today. Before the advent of radio, television and the Internet, people often used their rare leisure time reading the Bible, which could be found in just about every home. That probably accounts for the husband of Grace's Aunt Abigail going through life with the name Asahel. The pages of Grace's scrapbook were peppered with other unusual names, such as Etheyline, Azro, Sophronia and Zuba. Barzilla and Mehitabel was a couple who, it should come as no surprise, were the parents of Asahel.

Names like Relief and Ransom showed the strong evangelical influence in northern New England during the 1800s. The family of Grace Ladd was Christian Adventist, a group which had branched off from the teachings of William Miller, who preached during the 1830s and '40s that the Second Coming of Christ was imminent.

Many of the obituaries were clippings from the Adventist publications, **The World Crisis**, and gave insight into Adventist teachings about life and death. They believed that, at death, people were in an unconscious state until the coming of Christ, when the righteous would be resurrected to eternal life. The wicked were to experience eternal extinction (they rejected the doctrine of a fiery hell). Immersion was the method in which they consecrated their lives to Christ. Adventists referred to themselves as brothers and sisters and their religious leaders as elders. The obituary of Grace's Aunt Sarah, reads, "Sister Tuttle… rests waiting the coming of Him who has said, 'I am the resurrection and the life…' Words of comfort by Elder F.C. Young." They also espoused avoidance of tobacco and alcohol. Grace held to that creed even in her later years. One granddaughter recalls that she refused to drink the homemade root beer so popular on the farm during the hot summer weather because she objected to the word "beer."

The Advent influence in the North Country may explain several 19th century tombstones in Whitefield, including that of Elder Ira Bowles, which have engravings of fingers pointing down rather than up, indicating the person or soul is asleep in the grave until the resurrection at Christ's Advent. "Perhaps," writes Charles J. Jordan in his book, **Tales Told in the Shadows of the White Mountains**, "while all of his neighbors departed expecting that their spirits would be called upward in short order, Ira wanted the world to know that he was staying put and would only rise at the appointed time and not a minute sooner."

Besides tucking sermons in between a person's life story, obituary writers aired their observations about the character of the deceased with a freedom and frankness not possible in today's lawsuit-happy time. One wonders what Grace thought of these comments concerning an uncle: "Mr. (Orin) Hilliard was a man of very peculiar character," stated one such writer. "When his family were together he took comfort to himself." Another obituary reports," Warren Covell… of late had been out of his mind so that his family must have found it very hard to get along with him."

David Titus Noyes, a Boston Post Cane recipient, received this assessment: "He had ideas of his own and stood by them. He was faithful to his friends and had no use for those he did not like and left them severely alone."

These forthright and not-so-flattering comments were balanced with flowering compliments such as these: "Laura Barry...was a woman of rare loveliness of character, broad-minded and tolerant...generous to a fault, ever mindful of others and always doing the kindly acts which made her so universally beloved by all who knew her."

Mary Holden Kidder "was in most respects a model woman. We entertain no doubt concerning her destiny. She would be out of place anywhere else than in the presence of the pure and the good." And this one: "A better woman never breathed than Aunt Emily."

Honesty was a common theme, a trait admired by these ramrod-straight Yankees. Alma Cummings, editor and owner of the **News and Sentinel** for 25 years, earned this praise: "She was frank and outspoken, never evasive and could be depended on when her word was given."

The writers of Grace's day had a seemingly endless variety of ways of saying that someone had died. A farmer who collapsed on his way into town to deliver milk was said to have "died in the harness." A young girl's demise was described in this way: "Disease fastened itself upon her in early springtime and she faded as the leaf and flower in autumn." Others skipped the poetry and got right to the point. "David Allen Noyes is dead!" proclaimed one obituary.

Neither did writers shrink from providing detailed descriptions of a person's final moments on this earth. Perhaps it was their way of acknowledging the courage of the sufferers and the tenderness and sacrifices of their caretakers, who were mostly their mothers, sisters, daughters or wives rather than professional strangers. People usually entered and left this world at home with the help of their nearest and dearest.

The causes of death—from apoplexy, appendicitis, catarrhal fever and typhoid, are a time capsule of an era before antibiotics and the medical miracles possible with today's technology. One woman lost five of her children to diphtheria in a space of a few hours, followed by the death of two more sons and her husband.

Grace had numerous clippings of those who died young, perhaps out of fellow feeling. Two of Grace's children died very young. Two-year-old Earle died in 1897. In 1908, 21-year-old Ivo's windpipe was crushed by a kick from "a vicious horse" while working for lumber baron George Van Dyke's brother, T.H. Van Dyke, lingering three days before he died. Grace also lost a married daughter, Dencie Hunt (Beverly Uran's mother), to tuberculosis. Dencie left behind a large family of eight children.

"Words are cold things," wrote one of Grace's cousins, following Ivo's death, "but it's all we have." In that she may have been wrong. The words preserved in Grace Ladd's scrapbook are not cold, but warm, bringing to life the people of another century.

So are the images of Glenduen Wells Ladd, born at the "Turn of the Twentieth."

A 1922 photo of the Ladd farm on Piper Hill in Stewartstown, purchased by Grace Ladd's parents, Osmond and Susan Forrest, in 1870. Grace's letters, scrapbook and mementos representing over 60 years of North Country life and history, were stored in a trunk in an upper attic room near the chimney to the right. The farm remains in the hands of Grace's descendants. Glenduen Ladd photo.

The Nelson Ladd family sits stiffly for a formal shot: from left, Nelson, daughter Della, sons Ivo and Harry and wife Grace. The couple had eight children in all, including Fremont, Wesley, Earle, Dencie and Wayne. Author's collection.

On left, Dolly Aldrich, cousin to Harriet Beecher Stowe, with her husband, Bill; on right, Gad Beecher, founder of the Frontier Gazette. Grace Ladd collection.

When her youngest son, Earle, died at the age of two, Grace quietly tucked her grief away along with her son's nightshirt and baby rattle. The child's things were found carefully stored in a trunk in the Piper Hill farmhouse attic. Charles J. Jordan photo/Author's collection.

Also stored in the trunk were the contents of Grace's 21-year-old son Ivo's pockets at the time of his fatal accident at Tom Van Dyke's lumber camp. Charles J. Jordan photo/ Author's collection.

Glenduen (second from right) and friends in 1910.

The End

Printed in the United States
by Baker & Taylor Publisher Services